Folens RE Christianity

Contents

Christine Moorcroft

Daily Life

Sue Tyndall is a secretary. She works from Monday to Friday in a college. The charts show what she did on one weekday and on Sunday.

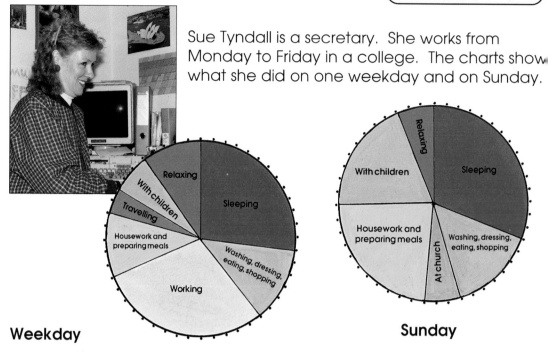

Weekday

Sunday

Dave Aldridge is an audio-visual aids technician. He looks after equipment such as projectors and televisions, takes photographs and does some filming.

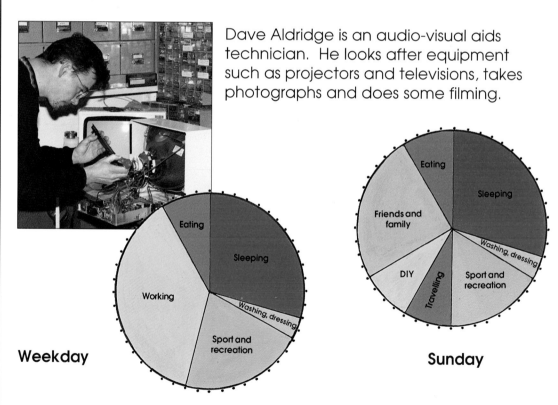

Weekday

Sunday

1   With a partner, list the things that Sue and Dave **have** to do and those that they do because they **want** to.

2   Explain any differences between their weekdays and Sundays.

3 Plan a survey to find out how people spend a typical weekday, Saturday and Sunday.

4 Record your findings. Make a diary for each person.

Name			
	Weekday	Saturday	Sunday
Morning			
Afternoon			
Evening			

You may need to change these times. Remember, do not speak to strangers.

Which activities serve other people?

Which activities serve God?

5 Talk to a partner about the activities of the people in your survey.

Which are just for the person himself or herself?

6 Classify the activities by using a chart like this:

	Serving others	Serving God	Serving self
Have to do			
Want to do			

7 Talk to a partner about your own activities and classify them in a similar way.

8 Which do you spend most time on, working or relaxing:
 - on Sundays?
 - on weekdays?
 - on Saturdays?
Explain the differences.

Working	Relaxing

So ... what have you learned about how much time people spend thinking about their religion?

Christianity

Sister Kathleen is a Roman Catholic nun. She works as a lecturer, training student teachers.

 1 How can you tell from the photographs that Sister Kathleen is a nun?

2 Why does she wear a cross?

Look at how Sister Kathleen spends some of her time.

3 Compare this to the diaries of people in your survey on page 3.

4 Compare it to the way the people on page 2 spend their time.

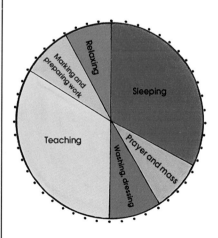

Weekday

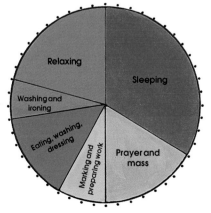

Sunday

4

Sister Kathleen lives with other nuns of the Notre Dame order.

The photograph shows the sisters just before a meal.

5   Explain what they are doing.

6   Why do some Christians do this before meals?

7   In groups, talk about prayers before meals. Then write your own prayer to be spoken before a special meal.

Think about ...

... how you will begin,
     ... who you are talking to,
        ... what you are thankful for,
           ... how you will finish the prayer.

What could you give thanks for, as well as for food?

8   Describe what you will do while you are praying.

9   Explain why you will do these things.

10   Does everyone in the group do the same thing? If not, why?

So ... what have you learned about how nuns show devotion to God and about prayer?

5

Christianity

Agnes Bojaxhiu was born in Skopje, in Macedonia. In 1928 she left her home and family, knowing she would never see them again, to become a nun, in Ireland and then in India. Whenever she could, she went into the streets of Calcutta to offer help and comfort to the poor.

One day Agnes, now called Sister Teresa, heard God calling her: "Give up everything and follow me into the slums to serve me among the poorest of the poor." So she trained as a nurse and set out with just a few coins, to start a school for the children of the slums. She knew that education is the only way to save children from the horror of poverty.

Children flocked to her, hungry for knowledge. As word spread of what she was doing people sent her gifts to help her with her work. She began to give out food and medicine as more and more people came to her for help. The building shown in the photograph came from these simple beginnings. Helpers gave up comfortable lives to join her in the never-ending work of caring for the poor. She was allowed to set up her own order of nuns, the Missionaries of Charity, who lived very simply and wore the clothes of poor women: thin white saris edged in blue.

Mother Teresa saw how the hospitals in Calcutta were bursting with sick people and had to turn away the poor and the dying. She knew then that she must make a place where they could turn to for help. She set up a home for orphaned, sick and abandoned children and started a hospital for people suffering from leprosy, a cruel disease that deforms and disfigures its victims.

More homes were opened and the work of Mother Teresa's order spread. There are now over three hundred houses across the world.

Mother Teresa has said that if all the meaning of Christianity had to be put into one word, this would be 'love'. In 1979 she was awarded the Nobel Peace Prize. In 1997 she died, aged 86.

Her Missionaries do not ask for anything in return for their work. Their homes are full of laughter and happiness and Mother Teresa has said that they are naturally happy because they are working for God.

People

"LET US DO SOMETHING BEAUTIFUL FOR GOD"

The Missionaries of Charity in Calcutta, India, founded by Mother Teresa.

What people need even more than food and shelter is to be wanted. Even if they have only a few hours left to live, they need to know that they are loved.
(Mother Teresa)

Try helping someone in need in your community, at work or at school. Begin by making whatever you do something beautiful for God.
(Mother Teresa)

Read what Mother Teresa said above.

 1 Describe how a poor or sick person might feel when visiting the place shown in the picture.

2 How do you think Mother Teresa and her helpers make sick people feel that they are loved and wanted?

 3 List some things that people you know have done that were 'something beautiful for God'.

So... what have you learned about why Mother Teresa chose the life that she followed?

Relationships

Many people support a local football team.

1 How can you tell which football team a group supports?

2 Copy the chart and use it to list words that could describe the feelings of football supporters.

Feelings of football supporters				
Before a match	During a match		After a match	
	Winning	Losing	Winners	Losers

3 Which feelings do you think make football supporters want to fight?

4 What could these people do instead of fighting?

5 Find out how football clubs help to stop crowd problems such as fighting.

Roman Catholics and Protestants are all Christians. Sometimes people from these two groups have fought with each other.

Catholic Priest MURDERED Retaliation feared

Peace Movement unites Catholic and Protestant Women

Catholic and Protestant war grows as family is killed

DEATH OF PROTESTANT CHILD IN TERRORIST EXPLOSION

6 Talk to friends about the violence described in these headlines. What do you think makes people do things like this?

7 If the people in the headlines obeyed the words of Jesus in **A**, what difference would it make?

8 Explain why it is sometimes difficult for Christians to obey the words of Jesus in **A**.

9 Draw a cartoon strip story that shows a Christian who follows the advice of Jesus.

A *But to you who hear me I say: Love your enemies; do good to those who hate you; bless those who curse you; pray for those who treat you spitefully. When a man hits you on the cheek, offer him the other cheek too ... Treat others as you would like them to treat you.*

(Luke 6: 27-31)

How would he or she feel after this?

How would he or she feel if someone tried to harm him or her?

What might he or she want to do at first?

...hat would he or she do?

So ... what have you learned about the Christian way of treating enemies?

Community

A community is a group of people who have the same interests.

 1 Look at the photographs. How can members of a community help each other?
Copy and complete this chart.

Community	Purpose	How the members can help each other
a		
b		
c		

2 With a partner, list some communities that you know.

3 How do their members help each other? Record your findings on a chart like the one above.

What is the purpose of these communities?

10

Cities, towns and villages have public places which belong to everybody. Sometimes people spoil these places.

4 How have the places in the pictures been spoiled by people?

5 Why do some people not look after public places?

6 Find out about some public places near where you live. Copy and complete the chart below.

What could you and your friends do to help keep public places pleasant?

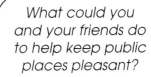

Public place	How people look after it	How people spoil it

7 Describe any times when you have seen someone spoiling a public place for others.

8 List some reasons why they do this.

So ... what have you learned about how you and other people can help each other?

Christian churches serve the people in their surrounding areas, or parishes.

   1   What do the people in this parish do together? Copy and complete the chart to help you organise your findings.

Activity	Age groups of people (M = Male, F = Female) (✔)											
	under 5		5-11		11-16		16-21		21-60		over 60	
	M	F	M	F	M	F	M	F	M	F	M	F

2   For which groups of people are there no activities?
What activities could be organised for these groups?

   3   Find out about the parish in which your school is situated. Look at a map to find out how big it is.

> *Take this and eat; this is my body ... Drink from it, all of you. For this is my blood the blood of the covenant, shed for many for the forgiveness of sins.*
> (Matthew 26: 26-29)

4 Look at the painting of the Last Supper. Do you think Jesus knew what was going to happen to him? Explain your answer.

A

5 Look at **A**. Describe what is being used in the Holy Communion service.

6 Read the words of a Holy Communion prayer in **B**. Explain it.

7 Find out what many Christians believe they are sharing during Holy Communion.

B *Almighty God, our heavenly Father. We have sinned against our fellow men in thought, word and deed, through negligence, through weakness, through our own deliberate fault. We are truly sorry and repent of all our sins.*

So ... what have you learned about Christian ideas of serving others and of Holy Communion?

Special Times

If you have a hamster as a pet, it will only live for about two years.

 1 The photograph shows a healthy hamster. How can you tell that it is alive? What will happen to it after it dies? Talk to your partner about any of your pets that have died.

 2 With friends, plan what you would do if a pet hamster died.

3 Write a short play about a pet hamster that dies.

Think about:

Scenes

Characters

What you will need

What they will

What they will say

When Christians die, their bodies are usually buried or cremated (burned). A stone or plaque is sometimes put up in memory of them.

4 Look at the words on the memorials. What do they tell you about the people who died and the people who want to remember them? Copy and complete the chart.

5 Christians hope to go to heaven, to be with God and Jesus when they die. Discuss this. Write a poem or draw a picture to show your idea of heaven.

	About the dead person: age, how he or she died, other information	Who will miss him or her	How they will remember him or her
a			
b			

Think about:

Where heaven is

How people get there

Who is there

What it is like there

What they are doing

15

Celebration

The photograph shows a happy carnival scene.

 1   How is carnival day different from ordinary days?
Copy and complete the chart.

Actions	Clothes	Food	Decorations	Sounds

2   How do people feel at festival time? Think about any
carnivals, festivals or fairs that you have been to.

Describe feelings: before the festival (preparing)
during the festival (taking part)
after the festival (getting back
to normal).

In Britain the poppy is used as a symbol to remember people who have died in wars. It was chosen because so many were growing in the fields of Northern France, where many soldiers died during the First World War.

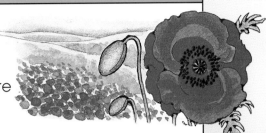

The photograph shows a Remembrance Day service on 11th November, when people wear poppies.

3 Describe the differences between this festival and the carnival.

4 Find out about a sad event that happened near where you live.

5 Describe how the event is remembered.
- What do people do?
- Has anything been built?
- Are any symbols used?

So ... what have you learned about different kinds of celebrations and how they are remembered?

Lent begins on Ash Wednesday and lasts for 40 days until Easter. The day before Ash Wednesday is Shrove Tuesday. 'Shrove' comes from a medieval word: 'shriven'. This means to be forgiven for sins that have been confessed.

Shrove Tuesday   **Ash Wednesday**

Many Christians go to Ash Wednesday church services. The priest puts ashes on their foreheads. These are a symbol to show that a person is trying to think of God rather than everyday things and will try to do good in the future.

1   Decide what day the words in **A** describe. Sort them using a copy of the chart. Which words could describe both pictures?

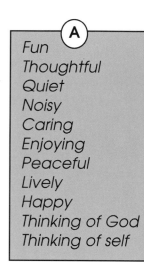

Fun
Thoughtful
Quiet
Noisy
Caring
Enjoying
Peaceful
Lively
Happy
Thinking of God
Thinking of self

Shrove Tuesday	Ash Wednesday

2   In groups, list some 'everyday' things that you could stop thinking about on Ash Wednesday.

3   Which would you find the most difficult to forget about?

4   Think of a good deed that you could do in the future. Talk to a partner about it.

Lent is a time when Christians remember the 40 days Jesus spent fasting in the wilderness. He thought only of God. You can read about it in the Bible in Matthew 4:1-11.

5 What is a wilderness like? Close your eyes and imagine it. Draw your wilderness.

6 Describe the sounds that you could hear there.

7 How would you feel if you were alone there?

List the things that you would think about in the wilderness.

Many Christians try to do without luxuries during Lent, just as Jesus gave up food for 40 days.

8 Find out about the luxuries enjoyed by others in your class. Are they things people really **need**, or are they just things people **want**?

9 Which luxury would you give up to help others?

10 Plan a way for your class to help others during Lent and at other times.

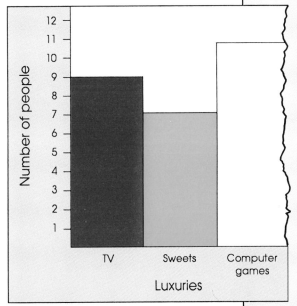

So ... **what have you learned about why and how Christians celebrate Lent?**

Special places

Look at the photographs of places that people think are special.

 1 Decide what is special about these places. Copy and complete the chart.

Place	Why it is special
a	
b	
c	

Places can be special for many reasons:
a. They hold beautiful things made by people.
b. Important decisions are made there.
c. People can go there for peace and quiet.

2 Use photographs and books or magazines to find a place that is special for you.

3 Explain your choice to a partner. What makes it special?

Places

20

...n and make a special ...lace in your school. Work with friends.

4 What is the special place for?

5 List some places where it could be made and decide which would be the best place.

6 Copy and use this chart to plan your special place.

Sketch what it will look like.	What it will sound like. (It could be silent.)
	How we will make the sounds, or make sure it is silent.
	Materials:

7 Talk about rules for using your special place.

How can we keep it special?

When can it be used?

Who will look after it?

Who can use it?

8 Write your rules in a way that makes them look special.

9 Make your special place.

So ... what have you learned about how to make and keep an ordinary place special?

Cathedrals are holy places. They are often designed to show the importance of God, that He is here forever, but that people are on the Earth for only a short time.

1   What do you notice about the size of the cathedral in the picture?

2   Think of some enormous places where you have been. How did you feel when you were there?

3   How does this cathedral show the importance of God?

4   List parts you think were the most difficult to make. List parts you think are the most beautiful. Explain your answers.

When a cathedral is built, only the best architects are asked to design it. Only the most skilful crafts people work on the cathedral. They use the best quality materials. A cathedral is a holy place, where Christians pray. It is also a monument to the glory of God.

5 Explain why such care is taken in the building of a cathedral.

6 Work with a partner. Choose the photograph that you both think shows that a cathedral is a holy place. Explain why you think this.

7 Which photograph best shows the glory of God? Explain why you think this.

So ... what have you learned about why a cathedral is a special place of worship for Christians?

Parulclient no

Creation

1   What does this photograph suggest about the size of the Earth and the size of the universe? Talk to a partner about your size and the size of the universe.

2   On a scale model, where you are the size of a full stop, what would you use to show the size of:
- your classroom
- your school
- your town
- your country
- the Earth
- the universe?

3   Find out how old the Earth is. Describe a graph that would show, to scale: your age, the age of your school, your town and the earth. Why would this be difficult to draw?

.. the earth was without form and void, with darkness over the face of the abyss, and a mighty wind that swept over the surface, of the waters. And God said, "Let there be light."

(Genesis 1:1-3)

4   Imagine that you can climb into the photograph. What can you see, hear, smell and feel?

5   Work with a partner. Describe what might have happened as God created day and night, Heaven and earth, the moon and stars.

6   List some words that describe a God who could do all this. Use them to write a poem.

Most Christians believe that in the beginning God created a perfect world.

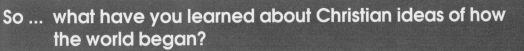

So ... what have you learned about Christian ideas of how the world began?

A long walk

People have to prepare themselves to go on journeys.
They may have many reasons for going.

1 Which of the items in the picture would be useful during a long walk? Copy and complete the chart.

Item	Use

2 Explain how each item would be useful.

3 You cannot take everything. Decide which items you would take on a long walk and which you would leave behind. Explain your choices.

4 List any essential items that are missing. Why are they essential for a long walk?

How do you feel when you are on your walk? Choose some of the words from the Word Bank.

Word Bank

excited
thoughtful
bored
healthy
tired
energetic
cheerful

Some people like to walk alone in quiet places. They leave everyday things behind. They like to be alone to think.

Diane enjoys the freedom and peace of a long walk. She likes to get away from the rush of too many things to do.

Dave thinks about the people he has walked with. Walks bring back happy memories.

5 Dave asks himself questions as he walks. With a friend, list some questions he might ask and think of some answers.

6 List some things that Diane might enjoy getting away from.

7 Explain how long walks might help people to think about important things.

Sometimes you need to be by yourself to concentrate on the important things in life.

So ... what have you learned about the value of being alone?

Christianity

Jesus travelled the Holy Land, spreading the word of God. He found many people who were sick, suffering and in need of help. He asked his disciples to travel separately, so that as many people as possible could be helped.

This is what Jesus said to the 12 disciples before they set off:

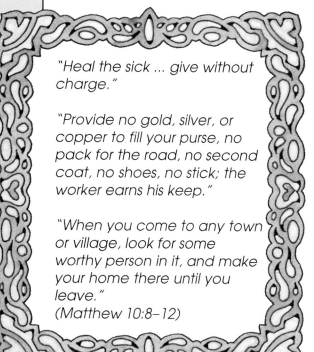

"Heal the sick ... give without charge."

"Provide no gold, silver, or copper to fill your purse, no pack for the road, no second coat, no shoes, no stick; the worker earns his keep."

"When you come to any town or village, look for some worthy person in it, and make your home there until you leave."
(Matthew 10:8–12)

1. Draw a large picture of the disciples setting off on their journey.

2. With a partner, talk about the things that might have worried the disciples as they set off. Write in speech bubbles some of the things they might have said. The speech bubbles should fit on to your drawing.

3. What did the disciples do for food, shelter and warm clothes during their travels?

4. Find out more about the 12 disciples and how they helped to spread the word of God.

Look in Matthew 10:2–4; Mark 3:16–19 and Luke 6:14–16.

Look carefully at the map and read about what happened on the journeys of Jesus.

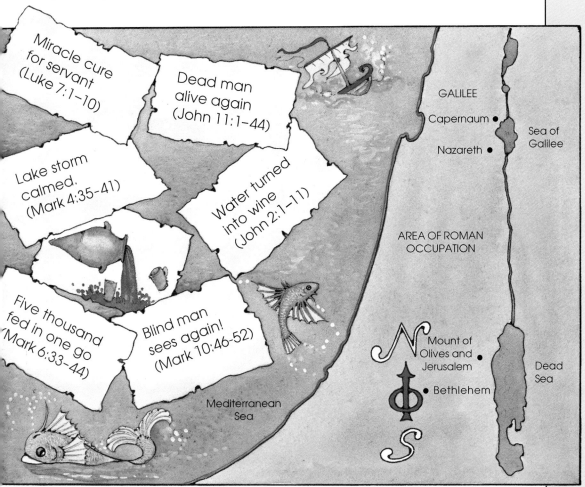

5   Copy and complete the chart.

Where	Who was involved	What happened	Bible reference

6   Find out about some more miraculous events that happened when Jesus and his disciples were travelling.

7   Find out about and retell some of the stories Jesus told on his travels.

So ... what have you learned about why Jesus and his disciples made journeys?

Journeys

Lourdes

People often make journeys to places where important things have happened, or famous people have lived or died.

Beatrix Potter, the author, lived in this cottage in Near Sawrey in the Lake District. People visit it each year.

The Beatles wrote and sang a song about Penny Lane in Liverpool. Tourists can be seen taking photographs of it nearly every day.

 1 What do you think people want to see in Beatrix Potter's cottage and garden?

2 What might people be thinking about when they visit Penny Lane?

 3 Find out about other places made famous by people or events. Copy and complete the chart.

Place	Person	Event
Near Sawrey	Beatrix Potter	
Penny Lane Liverpool	The Beatles	A song was written
Sherwood Forest		
Stratford-upon-Avon		

Every year thousands of Christians visit the shrine of Saint Bernadette in Lourdes, France.

4 Describe the people in the photograph.

5 Choose three people who might have different reasons for making the journey or pilgrimage to Lourdes. Describe their reasons for going.

List the things you will need to find out.

6 Work in a group. Plan a pilgrimage to Lourdes. Think about:
- how to get there
- how long it would take
- who else would go
- what you would take
- what you would do there
- the cost
- what you would think about there.

Where will you find this information?

7 Find out more about Saint Bernadette. Present your findings to another group.

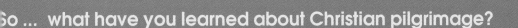

Ash Wednesday (18) The first day of **Lent**.

cathedral (22) An important church.

church (12) A building in which Christians worship.

confess (18) When Christians confess they tell God about the wrong things they have done and ask Him to forgive them.

Creation (24) When God made the world.

crucified (13) Killed by being nailed to a cross. This is how **Jesus** was put to death.

disciple (28) A follower and friend. According to the Bible, **Jesus** had twelve disciples.

heaven (15) Christians (and Jews and Muslims) call the kingdom of God heaven.

Holy Communion (13) A religious service during which Christians eat a piece of bread and drink some wine to symbolise the body and blood of Jesus. Some Christians believe that the bread and wine really become the body and blood of Jesus.

Holy Land (28) Middle Eastern countries, including Israel and Jordan, where the stories in the Bible took place.

Jesus (28) The most important person to Christians whom they worship. Believed to be the son of God.

Lent (18) The time when Christians remember the forty days Jesus spent fasting in the wilderness.

miracle (29) An amazing event which can not be rationally explained.

missionary (6) Someone who devotes his or her life to spreading the Christian faith.

Mother (6) The title given to a nun who is in charge of a convent or group of nuns.

nun (4) A woman who gives her life to serving God. Nuns can have jobs outside the convents where they live; these jobs are usually jobs which help others, such as teaching, medical work or social work. Their pay for their work is given to the **order** to which they belong.

order (5) A group to which nuns belong, such as the order of Notre Dame.

parish (12) The area served by a church.

pilgrimage (31) A religious journey.

saint (31) Someone who has shown great devotion to God; the title 'saint' is given after the person has died, and he or she might have a special day on which s/he is remembered.

sin (13) To do something wrong or bad.

Sister (4) The title given to a nun.